Praise for *When Wrong Seems Right*

This devotional is strategic and purposeful in its methodology, reflecting Griffin's background in education. Kids who go through this devotional will never just "read a Bible verse" again. Every lesson reinforces that God rarely says something just once; rather the Bible can be cross-referenced to get a fuller understanding of each verse. The way the questions are phrased trains kids to always be looking for connections between seemingly disparate passages. Comparing similarities is higher order thinking and will make youth dig deeper than the more commonly used "read and regurgitate" type questions. This book doesn't just teach the Bible. It teaches kids how to read, study, and integrate the Bible into their lives—and gives them permission to ask follow-up questions (which communicates to them that the church is a safe place for questions!). Well done, Adam! I'll be recommending this study to all my Mama Bears!

HILLARY MORGAN FERRER
President and founder of Mama Bear Apologetics; coauthor of *Mama Bear Apologetics: Empowering Your Kids to Challenge Cultural Lies* and *Mama Bear Apologetics Guide to Sexuality: Empowering Your Kids to Understand and Live Out God's Design*

It's not easy to write a book for kids that marries substance and simplicity, but Adam has brought the two together beautifully in this kid-friendly guide to God's guidance. These pages channel God's wisdom through a wise pastor to make wise kids.

DAVID MURRAY
Pastor of First Byron CRC; author of *Exploring the Bible* and *Meeting with Jesus*

Adam eloquently described the book of Proverbs as "God's gift of wisdom." Only Adam could unwrap that gift for kids in a way that encourages them, through questions, to discover God's path and a life well lived.

RON HUNTER JR.
Author and CEO of D6 Family Ministry

Adam's book is a great resource that will help children understand the beauty and value of the wisdom we receive from God. Through this study, he offers a concise and captivating overview of Proverbs and, along the way, helps children grow their Bible study skills. Parents and children alike will find this book to be a blessing!

ELIZABETH WOODSON
Author and Bible teacher

T0016590

When Wrong Seems Right is a very helpful, practical, and accessible introduction to the book of Proverbs. I'd recommend it to anyone who wants to grow in wisdom as they grow up!

REBECCA MCLAUGHLIN

Author of *Exploring the Earliest Gospel: A Kids Bible Study in the Book of Mark*, among other books

WHEN WRONG SEEMS RIGHT

A KIDS BIBLE STUDY ON

MAKING GOOD CHOICES

ADAM GRIFFIN

MOODY PUBLISHERS
CHICAGO

Edited by Amanda Cleary Eastep
Interior design: Faceout Studios, Paul Nielsen
Cover design: Brittany Schrock
Cover graphic of compass copyright © 2023 by 32 pixels/Adobe Stock (447756663). All rights reserved.

ISBN: 978-0-8024-2940-7

Printed by Versa Press in East Peoria, IL, September 2023

Originally delivered by fleets of horse-drawn wagons, the affordable paperbacks from D. L. Moody's publishing house resourced the church and served everyday people. Now, after more than 125 years of publishing and ministry, Moody Publishers' mission remains the same—even if our delivery systems have changed a bit. For more information on other books (and resources) created from a biblical perspective, go to www.moodypublishers.com or write to:

Moody Publishers
820 N. LaSalle Boulevard
Chicago, IL 60610

1 3 5 7 9 10 8 6 4 2

Printed in the United States of America

This is dedicated to my sons, Oscar, Gus, and Theodore,
who taught me that there's no such thing as too much fun.

I hope you'll always know right from wrong, boys.
Follow God no matter what.

CONTENTS

GETTING STARTED

Have you ever become separated from your family in a crowded place? It's scary to be alone in a crowd of strangers. It's also a little terrifying to try to decide what to do next. Do you stay where you are? Do you turn around and backtrack? Do you turn right or left? If you pick the wrong direction, you might be getting even farther away from your family. What is the right way to go?

Our whole lives can be like the decisions we make when we are lost and alone. There is a right way to go in life, but if we just follow our instincts and do what feels right, we may find ourselves going the wrong way. You might start going in a direction that is taking you farther from where God wants you. Instead of following a path that honors God, you may choose things that are sinful—bad for you and offensive to God.

Where do we turn when we want to know what to do?

The book of Proverbs in the Bible is God's gift of wisdom to His people. Wisdom is knowing how to find and follow God. Even if you are convinced some other way is better, following God's wisdom is always, *always* the right way to go. There's no better place to find wisdom than in the Bible because the Bible comes from a God who loves you and knows better than you do what is good for you.

How to Read *This* Book

At the beginning of each day's lesson in this study of God's Word, you'll **read a short proverb** from the book of Proverbs and then **answer some questions** about it.

You'll also **find a New Testament cross-reference** to look up. A cross-reference is a verse that is somewhere else in the Bible but relates to the verse you're studying. These verses from the New Testament will help you better understand the proverbs you're studying so you can gain the wisdom God has for you.

We also want you to **learn how to ask questions about the text** you are reading and be able to find other verses in the Bible that help you answer your questions. In the back of many Bibles is a concordance. It is kind of like a glossary or list of topics and important words and where they are found in the Bible. For instance, if you wanted to find verses that can comfort you when you're scared, you would look up "fear" or "courage" in the concordance, and it would give you a list of verses to look up.

You'll learn to use this tool as you learn to study your Bible and find answers to your questions. If you don't have access to a Bible with a concordance, ask a parent or teacher who loves God to help you answer your questions. Or use an online tool like BibleGateway.com to find additional verses to guide you.

God's Directions

Not knowing the right thing to do is a really tough spot to be in. Sometimes knowing right from wrong is harder than you think. That's why we all need the loving wisdom offered in Proverbs. I hope that as you study this book of the Bible you will grow in wisdom. I also hope you grow in confidence that God loves you even if you have made the worst possible choices in the past. God is gracious to people who have gone the wrong way, but He also loves us enough to give us better directions. **God's ways will always be better than trusting our sinful hearts.**

Being guided by God's wisdom is great, but it's not even the best part of the Bible we are about to study together. You see, no matter how hard people try to always make the best choice, we will eventually (and perpetually) make poor choices. We will all figure out that we went "the wrong way." That's why the story of God's grace offered to you in Jesus Christ is the absolute best news.

While sin is always serious, God's grace is always greater! There is not a mistake that we could make that can't be forgiven and corrected through the love of Jesus Christ. God's Son gave His life to take on the consequences of all our mistakes. Because of that, those of us who trust in Jesus get to walk free, declared righteous in Jesus, no matter what our sins are—past, present, or future.

WEEK 1

— WISDOM —

WHAT'S WISE?

WAYS THAT SEEM RIGHT

> *There is a way that seems right to a man,*
> *but its end is the way to death.*
>
> PROVERBS 14:12

If you own a dog, you may know chocolate is toxic to them. Chocolate is something people eat as a treat, and many dogs will gladly gobble it up if they can get their paws on it. Unfortunately, this sweet dessert is poisonous and potentially deadly for your canine friends.

God tells us that it isn't always easy to know what is good for us. Some things that appear to be good or "neutral" (not obviously good or bad) to us might actually be harmful. Things like songs, books, movies, or shows might seem harmless, but if they teach something opposed to God's teaching, they can lead us astray or distract us from what is good. It is really important to know who to trust when you want to decide whether something is wrong or right. You can't just trust your instincts or desires because harmful things will often seem good to you.

If you are sick, you trust a doctor to advise you on how to get better. To pass a test at school, you trust your teacher to prepare you. To live a godly life, you shouldn't trust what anyone says is good unless it lines up with what God says. Christians don't follow the crowd unless the crowd is following Jesus. Even if everyone else we know is convinced something is right, and even if it seems right to us, if God says it is wrong, we will trust Him only.

The unbelieving people around us will tell us how normal and harmless some choices are. But the Bible would call those same choices selfish, immoral, dishonest, and sinful. As we get to know God and His Word, we will know better. God's Word helps us "discern" what's best. Discerning is the God-given ability to tell what is right from what is wrong.

As hard as it might be, we should stand up for what is right because we trust the all-knowing God over people's opinions.

1. Can you think of a time when your parents helped you see that something you did wasn't the best option for you?

_____

_____

_____

2. Why is it hard to believe something when other people disagree with you?

_____

_____

_____

3. Why do you think some things that are wrong seem right to us?

_____

_____

_____

Read Matthew 7:13–14. (This is a cross-reference, another verse in the Bible that is related to the one we are studying.)

4. How are these words from Jesus related to Proverbs 14:12?
(Reminder: this is the verse at the beginning of the lesson.)

_____

_____

_____

5. *After reading these two passages, write out three questions you have about these verses.* (Questions might be something like: Why doesn't God just make me want what's good? Or, How do I know if I'm on the narrow, or right, path?)

1. _____
   _____
   _____

2. _____
   _____
   _____

3. _____
   _____
   _____

6. *What other verses in the Bible help to answer your questions?* (Reminder: use the concordance in the back of your Bible or ask a grown-up who loves God and reads the Bible.)

_____
_____
_____

7. *What do you think is the most important idea of these two passages, Matthew 7:13–14 and Proverbs 14:12?*

_____
_____
_____

8. *What do these verses ask or inspire you to think, feel, or do?*

_____

_____

_____

_____

_____

_____

_____

FINDING TREASURE

> *Blessed is the one who finds wisdom,*
> *and the one who gets understanding,*
> *for the gain from her is better than gain from*
> *silver and her profit better than gold.*
> *She is more precious than jewels,*
> *and nothing you desire can compare with her.*
>
> PROVERBS 3:13–15

Which is greater, a nickel or a dime? It depends, right? It's not that easy of a question. If you are talking about weight or size, a nickel is greater. If you are talking about monetary value, a dime is worth twice as much. Wouldn't it be foolish if someone wanted to trade dimes for nickels?

What is worth more to you, gold or wisdom? In other words, would you rather be wealthy or wise?

You can be the richest person in the world, but if you make foolish choices or act foolishly, you will hurt yourself and hurt others. You can be the smartest kid in your class, but if you only use your intelligence to make fun of people or so you can slack off in class, is your brilliance that valuable? If you are strong or fast or artistic or talented but you don't know the difference between right and wrong, then your skills won't end up helping you or anyone else.

God's Word says that wisdom is more valuable than gold, silver, and jewels. God is saying that knowing Him and trusting Him in how to live rightly is the most valuable thing you could seek in your life. Knowing the proverbs will help you do that. The understanding you'll gain will be more valuable than a treasure chest full of gold.

1. What is the most valuable thing your mom or dad has ever taught you?

_____

_____

_____

2. What is your most valuable possession? If you lost it, how hard would you look for it?

_____

_____

_____

3. Is there anyone in your life who seems godly and wise to you? A parent? A teacher or coach? An aunt or uncle? What questions do you think they could help you answer to help you "find wisdom"?

_____

_____

_____

Read Matthew 13:44–46.

4. How are these words from Jesus about treasure similar to the treasures in Proverbs 3:13–15?

_____

_____

_____

5. After reading these two passages, write out three questions you have about these verses.

1. _____

_____

_____

2. _____

_____

_____

3. _____

_____

_____

6. What other verses in the Bible help to answer your questions?

_____

_____

_____

7. What do you think is the most important idea of these two passages, Matthew 13:44–46 and Proverbs 3:13–15?

_____

_____

_____

8. What do these verses ask or inspire you to think, feel, or do?

_____

_____

_____

_____

YOU OBEY WHAT YOU FEAR

> *The fear of the Lord is the beginning of knowledge;*
> *fools despise wisdom and instruction.*
>
> PROVERBS 1:7

The first time I saw a whale shark, I was standing against the glass of an enormous aquarium. Suddenly a spotted creature of unbelievable size glided slowly by, just a few feet in front of me. It was truly unnerving. I was in no danger, and whale sharks don't even eat people (or so they say), but it was so big that I was a little shaken by the experience.

The beginning of wisdom, or the start of not being a fool, is understanding that God is wiser than you are. The fear of God is the awesome recognition that God is powerful and wise beyond all of your comprehension. That's even more amazing than a whale shark swimming right in front of your face.

If you want to be wise, that starts with understanding that God knows better than you. Not just about some things; God knows better than you about everything. That is part of what makes Him God and makes you you. You need God. He does not need you, but in His love for you, He grants you His wisdom. Proverbs is full of knowledge and wisdom for you, and you need all of it. Not everyone loves and trusts God, but the people who *do* love, fear (honor and revere), and trust God are truly wise.

1. What situation have you gone through where you were grateful and glad that your mom or dad was with you?

_____

_____

_____

2. How do you know that God is wiser than you?

_____

_____

_____

3. How do we get wisdom from God?

_____

_____

_____

Read John 3:18–21.

4. Proverbs 1:7 and John 3:18–21 talk about the benefits of trusting God. What are those benefits according to these verses?

_____

_____

_____

5. After reading these two passages, write out three questions you have about these verses.

1. _____

_____

_____

2. _____

_____

_____

3. _____

_____

_____

6. *What other verses in the Bible help to answer your questions?*

_____

_____

_____

_____

7. *What do you think is the most important idea of these two passages, John 3:18–21 and Proverbs 1:7?*

_____

_____

_____

8. *What do these verses ask you to think, feel, or do?*

_____

_____

_____

_____

FOOLISHNESS

> *Whoever loves discipline loves knowledge,*
> *but he who hates reproof is stupid.*
>
> PROVERBS 12:1

Have you ever made a mistake that made you feel foolish? I've done it countless times. Once, when I was little, I thought there was an alien outside my bedroom window that I was sure was trying to abduct me. I told my mom about it several times before she finally opened my curtains to show me that the voice I was hearing was from a restaurant drive-thru window nearby. Having someone who knew better about what was happening sure solved my alien problems quick.

God has given you a lot of people in your life He has tasked with disciplining and correcting you. When a parent, teacher, or pastor gently addresses areas of your life where you have something to learn, their guidance will help you grow in wisdom, faith, and godliness. If, however, you ignore the wisdom of trustworthy and godly adults, the Bible would call that foolishness.

God isn't silent about what is right, and you should trust Him over your own heart 100 percent of the time. To ignore God's commands in order to follow your own desires is truly foolish.

1. What lesson that your mom or dad taught you has made a big difference in your life?

_____

_____

_____

2. What is something that God has asked you to do that is hard for you?

_____

_____

_____

3. What is the best advice or correction you've ever received from someone?

_____

_____

_____

Read Ephesians 5:15–17.

4. In Ephesians 5, Paul says that knowing God's will keeps you from being foolish. How does that relate to Proverbs 12:1?

_____

_____

_____

5. After reading these two passages, write out three questions you have about these verses.

1. _____

_____

_____

2. _____

_____

_____

3. _____

_____

_____

6. What other verses in the Bible help to answer your questions?

_____

_____

_____

_____

7. What do you think is the most important idea of these two passages, Ephesians 5:15–17 and Proverbs 12:1?

_____

_____

_____

8. What do these verses ask you to think, feel, or do?

_____

_____

_____

_____

WHO TO TRUST

*Trust in the L*ord *with all your heart,
and do not lean on your own understanding.
In all your ways acknowledge him,
and he will make straight your paths.
Be not wise in your own eyes;
fear the L*ord*, and turn away from evil.*

PROVERBS 3:5–7

The first time I got a flat tire, I was seventeen years old and going 75 miles per hour on a highway in the middle of nowhere. I made it safely to the shoulder of the road, but I had no idea how to remove a flat tire and put on a spare tire. I tried for an hour to get the spare out from under my van. Fortunately, a man in a tow truck stopped and helped me out. It took him less than a minute to get access to my spare tire.

The difference between him and me was not strength, it was understanding. He knew exactly what to do, and I had no idea. Honestly, if I would've taken one minute to read the instruction manual in my glove compartment, I could have done it myself. But I didn't even know to do that.

God warns us that if you go through life leaning only on your own understanding, you will end up on a wrong path. He graciously offers to give us His understanding to guide us through life. Assuming that you will be able to trust yourself and your understanding about what is best is called "being wise in our own eyes." To think you know better than God does about what is right is to follow a path away from God.

Thankfully, you have a God who has offered to come along and rescue you from your own lack of understanding. Trusting Him with your life leads to a straight path that turns away from evil.

1. *How have your mom and dad helped you know who to trust?*

_____

_____

_____

2. *When was a time that you needed someone else's help because you didn't know how to solve your own problem?*

_____

_____

_____

3. *How can someone get wisdom from God on what is right and wrong?*

_____

_____

_____

Read 1 Corinthians 3:18–20.

4. *Read Proverbs 3:5–7 again. According to these two passages, what makes God different than us?*

_____

_____

_____

5. *After reading these two passages, write out three questions you have about these verses.*

1. _____

_____

_____

2. _____

_____

_____

3. _____

_____

_____

6. *What other verses in the Bible help to answer your questions?*

_____

_____

_____

_____

_____

_____

7. *What do you think is the most important idea of these two passages,*
1 Corinthians 3:18–20 and Proverbs 3:5–7?

_____

_____

_____

8. *What do these verses ask you to think, feel, or do?*

_____

_____

_____

_____

_____

WEEK 2

— VIRTUES —

WHAT'S RIGHT?

HUMILITY

> *The reward for humility and fear of the Lord*
> *is riches and honor and life.*
>
> PROVERBS 22:4

This is a good example of a proverb that is a principle but not a promise. God is not saying that if you are humble He promises you wealth. He *is* saying that it's better and more rewarding to be humble than to be self-centered. It's generally true that selfishness doesn't lead to having what's best or having true strength. People who don't trust God think it's greater to get what you want, do what you want, and be served rather than serving others. This isn't true for those who follow God.

Humility is a character quality you should expect to see in a Christian. It takes humility to trust that God knows best. What God says is good for you may not always seem right to you. God knows that considering the needs of others is better than always getting what you want. You don't have to dislike yourself to be humble. That's not God's will.

Humility looks like valuing others so much that it is a delight to serve them. It looks like being so confident of God's love for you that you don't need to seek affirmation from other people in order to feel good about yourself. You don't need to earn trophies or the highest grades or the coolest friends or the attention of other people to feel good. You don't need to defeat your peers at something to be happy.

Our world says we should chase attention and popularity, but Christ says our greatest reward comes from being a servant. Whether that's letting someone else go ahead of us, cleaning up someone else's mess, or just doing what we're supposed to without being asked again by our parents, finding ways to humbly serve is always a wise choice.

1. When have you seen your mom or dad serve your family?

_____

_____

_____

2. Why do you think it's hard for us to enjoy serving other people more than being served?

_____

_____

_____

3. Do you know someone who is really humble? How do they show that they are humble?

_____

_____

_____

Read Mark 10:42–45.

4. How is Jesus' description of a servant leader related to Proverbs 22:4?

_____

_____

_____

_____

5. *After reading these two passages, write out three questions you have about these verses.*

1. _____
   _____
   _____

2. _____
   _____
   _____

3. _____
   _____
   _____

6. What other verses in the Bible help to answer your questions?

_____
_____
_____

7. What do you think is the most important idea of these two passages, Mark 10:42–45 and Proverbs 22:4?

_____
_____
_____

8. What do these verses ask or inspire you to think, feel, or do?

_____
_____
_____

JOY OR DESPAIR

> *A joyful heart is good medicine,*
> *but a crushed spirit dries up the bones.*
>
> PROVERBS 17:22

I went with some of my best friends from church once to see a comedian. By the end of the night, my face hurt from smiling for so long, and my eyes stung from laughing until I cried. The comedian was hilarious, and the experience felt fantastic. Whether it's laughing with friends, enjoying good food, winning a sports match, or getting a gift you didn't know you wanted, enjoying life really does bless a person.

Joy is actually something you can have even when circumstances are tough. You can rejoice that God is in control even when something awful happens. You can choose to have joy even when you are disappointed. Joy is rooted in our hope, and unlike those who don't serve God, no one can pry hope from the heart of believers in Jesus.

You would think that no one would ever choose to be sad, but the truth is that moping, complaining, grumbling, and pouting are often things many of us choose to do in response to our circumstances. Our hearts love to feel pity for ourselves. God encourages us, even in our darkest moments, that choosing joy over sulking is always better for us. Joy is also rooted in the reality that no circumstance can take from you all that you have in Christ. God is never cruel, and everything He does in your life matters. While we're not promised that life will be easy, we are promised that God will always be with us, and He is always good.

1. What is the funniest thing you've heard your mom or dad say?

_____

_____

_____

2. When you are tempted to sulk or pout, how do you break yourself out of that to choose joy?

_____

_____

_____

3. Why can Christians have joy regardless of their circumstances?

_____

_____

_____

Read Philippians 4:4–7.

4. According to Philippians 4:4–7 and Proverbs 17:22, how should our circumstances affect our joy?

_____

_____

_____

5. After reading these two passages, write out three questions you have about these verses.

1. _____

_____

_____

2. _____

_____

_____

3. _____

_____

_____

6. What other verses in the Bible help to answer your questions?

_____

_____

_____

_____

7. What do you think is the most important idea of these two passages, Philippians 4:4–7 and Proverbs 17:22?

_____

_____

_____

_____

8. What do these verses ask you to think, feel, or do?

_____

_____

_____

_____

INTEGRITY

> *The wicked flee when no one pursues,*
> *but the righteous are bold as a lion.*
>
> PROVERBS 28:1

If you have ever walked through the woods alone at night, you might know the feeling of intense fear that comes from feeling like you are being hunted or watched—even though you know (or at least you are pretty sure) nothing is out there. There's a similar fear that comes with having done something wrong and wondering if you are about to be caught.

If you steal something, even if no one has noticed your wrongdoing, you might feel as if you're in full panic escape mode and capture is around every turn. On the other hand, if something gets stolen and you're innocent, you can be "bold as a lion." You have nothing to fear because you did nothing wrong.

Being righteously bold is a privilege that comes with being right and doing right. You can be confident and courageous even when someone stands against you if you know that you're innocent. Of course, no one is perfect. But the sinning Christian can still be bold about right living because we are willing to admit our mistakes and ask for forgiveness.

Christians do not surrender to sin, nor do we hide it. Just because you struggle doesn't mean you give up. Just because you feel grief over sin doesn't mean you should run to shame. Be bold about what you know to be right, be innocent of wrongdoing; and where you fail, be bold enough to take responsibility for your actions. That is the way of the boldly righteous man or woman of God.

1. When have you seen your mom or dad make a choice to do the right thing even if it wasn't popular?

_____

_____

_____

_____

2. Why is it so easy to lose confidence that what you are doing is the right thing or to give up on trying to do good?

_____

_____

_____

_____

3. When have you felt shame driving you to hide something you've done rather than admit it?

_____

_____

_____

_____

Read Acts 4:1–13.

4. Where do you see boldness in this story about Peter and John being arrested, and how does that relate to Proverbs 28:1?

_____

_____

_____

_____

5. After reading these two passages, write out three questions you have about these verses.

1. _____

_____

_____

2. _____

_____

_____

3. _____

_____

_____

6. What other verses in the Bible help to answer your questions?

_____

_____

_____

7. What do you think is the most important idea of these two passages, Acts 4:1–13 and Proverbs 28:1?

_____

_____

_____

8. What do these verses ask you to think, feel, or do?

_____

_____

_____

SELF-CONTROL

> *A man without self-control*
> *is like a city broken into and left without walls.*
>
> PROVERBS 25:28

Have you ever had to wear a helmet when you ride a bike? Do you wear a seat belt when you ride in a car? I sure hope you do. Not taking certain precautions can put you at risk of serious injury . . . or worse. A city without walls can be at risk too because it is unprotected from enemies. That is what it's like to lack self-control. It's risky and hazardous. Your heart and mind are unprotected from the world and your enemy, the devil.

Having self-control means that, as Christians, we aren't forced to obey our sinful desires. We aren't slaves to sin. Self-control is a fruit of the Holy Spirit. If, however, you just do whatever seems right to you and continue to live with sinful desires as your master instead of following Jesus as Lord, you should not be surprised when you suffer the consequences of having weak defenses.

God gives you strength to face temptations and choose what is good. The gift of self-control is given to bless you. You don't have to do the sinful things that seem right to you. In Christ, we throw off that sin that so easily entangles and pursue a better way to live—God's way.

1. What are ways that you've seen your mom or dad protect you?

_____

_____

_____

2. What are things you are tempted to do that you know would be dangerous for you physically, emotionally, or spiritually?

_____

_____

_____

3. How is self-control a gift to you when you face temptations?

_____

_____

_____

Read 2 Timothy 1:7.

4. How is self-control portrayed differently in 2 Timothy 1:7 and Proverbs 25:28?

_____

_____

_____

5. After reading these two passages, write out three questions you have about these verses.

   1. _____

      _____

      _____

2. _____

_____

_____

3. _____

_____

_____

6. *What other verses in the Bible help to answer your questions?*

_____

_____

_____

_____

7. *What do you think is the most important idea of these two passages,*
2 Timothy 1:7 and Proverbs 25:28?

_____

_____

_____

8. *What do these verses ask you to think, feel, or do?*

_____

_____

_____

_____

WHEN TO CHEAT

> *Better a little with righteousness*
> *than much gain with injustice.*
>
> PROVERBS 16:8 NIV

There was a time in my life when I was a high school English teacher. For one of our assignments, my students had to write a sonnet. A sonnet is a fancy poem that follows certain rules for length and rhyme. One of my students turned in a magnificent poem. It was truly wonderful. In fact, it was too good. I plugged a few of his lines into a search engine on my computer, and seconds later I could see that he had copied his poem straight off the internet. His explanation to me was that it was a test to see if I actually read his homework. Really, it was just cheating. He was being dishonest in order to get what he wanted— less work and better grades.

God says it would be better to get a "little" and do it the right way than to get something great the wrong way. In other words, it would be better to get a bad grade than to cheat for a good one. It is better to make a little money doing an honest job than to be dishonest in an attempt to become rich.

Our sinful world will teach you that as long as "no one will know" or "no one will really get hurt," then it's okay to be dishonest for personal gain. If you're going to follow Jesus then you will be committing to not take from, or deceive, anyone no matter the gain, even if you can "get away" with it. The crowd may tell you that it's okay to trick a teacher or a classmate or your parents. When you're walking in wisdom, potential gains are never an excuse for dishonesty.

1. How would you feel if your mom or dad stole from you because they thought you wouldn't notice?

_____

_____

_____

2. How can having less really be better than having more?

_____

_____

_____

3. Why does God care if we are dishonest if no one is going to notice?

_____

_____

_____

Read 1 Timothy 6:6–9.

4. How does Proverbs 16:8 relate to the contentment Paul talks about in 1 Timothy 6:6–9?

_____

_____

_____

5. After reading these two passages, write out three questions you have about these verses.

1. _____

_____

_____

_____

2. _____

_____

_____

3. _____

_____

_____

6. *What other verses in the Bible help to answer your questions?*

_____

_____

_____

_____

7. *What do you think is the most important idea of these two passages,*
1 Timothy 6:6–9 and Proverbs 16:8?

_____

_____

_____

8. *What do these verses ask you to think, feel, or do?*

_____

_____

_____

_____

WEEK 3

— VICES —

WHAT'S WRONG?

FURY IS NOT YOUR FRIEND

> *Whoever is slow to anger has great understanding,*
> *but he who has a hasty temper exalts folly.*
>
> PROVERBS 14:29

Have you ever been really glad that you got mad? Have you ever been proud of losing your temper? Has anger ever served you better than patience? God says that the person who loves getting angry loves foolishness.

I know a man who lost one of his best friends because they got into an argument about whether his friend was out at second base during a baseball game. Did you hear that? He lost his very best friend because they got so angry about who was right in a silly game.

Anger is often rooted in not getting what you want when you want it. Our hearts love to win and love to be right. Sadly, the loudest, the meanest, and the one who bullies others in the room often gets their way. If you follow God's wisdom, you will not threaten or manipulate others to win an argument. Losing your temper might feel justified sometimes, it may even feel like the best way to get what you want, but God reminds us that patience comes from trusting God in every situation.

God has not just forgiven Christians; He has called us to be a people who forgive in the same way when we've been wronged. Remember, we have all wronged God. If anyone is justified in their anger, it's God. Instead of raging at you, though, He is patient with you. And He calls you to be patient and forgiving too.

1. When have you seen your mom or dad be patient instead of angry?

_____

_____

_____

2. Can you think of a time when you lost your temper over something?

_____

_____

_____

3. When you're tempted to be angry, what strategies do you have to calm yourself down?

_____

_____

_____

Read Ephesians 4:31–32.

4. What do Ephesians 4:31–32 and Proverbs 14:29 tell you to "get rid of"?

_____

_____

_____

5. After reading these two passages, write out three questions you have about these verses.

1. _____

_____

_____

_____

2. _____

_____

_____

3. _____

_____

_____

6. What other verses in the Bible help to answer your questions?

_____

_____

_____

_____

7. What do you think is the most important idea of these two passages, Ephesians 4:31–32 and Proverbs 14:29?

_____

_____

_____

8. What do these verses ask you to think, feel, or do?

_____

_____

_____

_____

_____

ARROGANCE

> *Do you see a person wise in their own eyes?*
> *There is more hope for a fool than for them.*
>
> PROVERBS 26:12

Has someone ever told you that you could "achieve anything you put your mind to"? That you could grow up to be "whatever you want"? That all you have to do is "believe in yourself"? All these things sound really kind and encouraging. Our world loves to say things like this to kids, and these sentiments seem right. Unfortunately, they feed into the dangerous lie that we don't think highly enough of ourselves or believe in ourselves enough. If anything, our problems come from thinking about ourselves *too* much.

A person's biggest problem is sin, and we can't solve sin. You need a Savior. Your biggest problem would be solved, not by believing more in yourself, but by believing and trusting in Jesus.

I hope you do have a bright future and that you have a lot of confidence that comes from God. I care about you and don't want to lie to you about your dreams. The key to unlocking your dreams and goals is not self-centered confidence. The wisest kid is not the one who assumes they already have everything they need inside of them to succeed. The wisest kid recognizes that they will always need more wisdom. You will always have more to learn, and you can learn from others and from God's Word if you aren't already wise in your own eyes.

1. When have you seen your mom or dad learning something from someone else?

_____

_____

_____

2. Why would being "wise in your own eyes" make it hard to learn something new?

_____

_____

_____

3. What makes us want to be great?

_____

_____

_____

Read Luke 9:46–48.

4. Compare the argument the disciples are having in Luke 9:46–48 to Proverbs 26:12.

_____

_____

_____

5. After reading these two passages, write out three questions you have about these verses.

1. _____

_____

_____

2. _____

_____

_____

3. _____

_____

_____

6. *What other verses in the Bible help to answer your questions?*

_____

_____

_____

_____

7. *What do you think is the most important idea of these two passages, Luke 9:46–48 and Proverbs 26:12?*

_____

_____

_____

8. *What do these verses ask you to think, feel, or do?*

_____

_____

_____

_____

_____

GRUMBLE. GRUMBLE. GRUMBLE

> *A fool gives full vent to his spirit,*
> *but a wise man quietly holds it back.*
>
> PROVERBS 29:11

I am so sick and tired of people complaining! I can't stand it when someone whines about what they want or grumbles about what they have to do. It gets on my nerves having to listen to someone voice their critical, bellyaching protests! *Arghhh!*

See what I did there? Complaining about complaining? Whining about whining? Critiquing the critics? I even threw in an "argh"!

It's really easy to be critical. Complaining comes to us very naturally. In most things, it's easier to tear down than to build up. Proverbs warns us that venting all of our negative thoughts is foolish. It helps no one, even ourselves, to share our selfish grumbling. It actually only makes things worse.

I hope that the man or woman of God you grow into is wise enough not to voice every complaint. I also hope that there is no room in your heart for the kind of negativity that leads to whining and complaining. God has called you to a better form of contentment. In Christ, we can be at peace and confident no matter what comes.

1. How have you seen your parents be patient with you even when you're complaining?

_____

_____

_____

2. Why do you think whining is foolish?

_____

_____

_____

3. How would refusing to complain make you different from most kids?

_____

_____

_____

Read Philippians 2:14–16.

4. Compare Proverbs 29:11 and Philippians 2:14–16. How are they alike, and how are they different?

_____

_____

_____

5. After reading these two passages, write out three questions you have about these verses.

1. _____

_____

_____

_____

2. _____

   _____

   _____

3. _____

   _____

   _____

6. *What other verses in the Bible help to answer your questions?*

_____

_____

_____

7. *What do you think is the most important idea of these two passages, Philippians 2:14–16 and Proverbs 29:11?*

_____

_____

_____

8. *What do these verses ask you to think, feel, or do?*

_____

_____

_____

_____

_____

MESSING UP OVER AND OVER

> *Like a dog that returns to his vomit*
> *is a fool who repeats his folly.*
>
> PROVERBS 26:11

This is absolutely one of the grossest verses in the Bible. But it is so true. What it means is that sometimes the mistakes you make, you will make again. And that, friend, is foolish. If you already know what it's like to make a sinful choice, you would hope that you'd never make that same one again. If you used your words to hurt, stole something, or lied to someone you love, you'd hope to never repeat those mistakes.

Sadly, human beings are prone to temptation. Even though you know better, you will sometimes repeat your errors. Something you know you shouldn't do, you may do more than once. Something you know you should do, you may ignore repeatedly.

Here's the good news. First, the Lord is eternally patient and never runs out of love and forgiveness for you! You can't make a mistake "one too many times" for Him to forgive you. Second, there is never a better time than right now to learn from your mistakes and resolve to never repeat them. There will be things in this world that seem right, but once you've learned they are not, quit them. That's why Jesus teaches us to pray, "Lead us not into temptation and deliver us from evil." That's my prayer for you too!

1. What is something your mom or dad does well that you could learn from?

_____

_____

_____

2. What is something you have gotten into trouble for more than once?

_____

_____

_____

3. What does God's forgiveness mean to you?

_____

_____

_____

Read Romans 7:15–19.

4. Compare and contrast how Romans 7:15–19 and Proverbs 26:11 talk about repeating our mistakes.

_____

_____

_____

5. After reading these two passages, write out three questions you have about these verses.

1. _____

_____

_____

_____

2. _____

_____

_____

3. _____

_____

_____

6. *What other verses in the Bible help to answer your questions?*

_____

_____

_____

_____

7. *What do you think is the most important idea of these two passages, Romans 7:15–19 and Proverbs 26:11?*

_____

_____

_____

8. *What do these verses ask you to think, feel, or do?*

_____

_____

_____

_____

_____

WHAT YOU SAY REALLY MATTERS

> *Death and life are in the power of the tongue,*
> *and those who love it will eat its fruits.*
>
> PROVERBS 18:21

I can remember many times when something that someone said made me sad, made me angry, or gave me a feeling in my chest like I'd been punched. I can also think of times where something someone said cheered me up, inspired me, changed the course of my life, or convinced me of a truth important to my life.

Words are incredibly powerful. I cringe thinking about how things that I've said, with very little thought, have made a really awful impact on someone else's life. It's a great comfort knowing, though, that maybe something I've said truly encouraged someone and has had a lasting positive effect.

What you say really matters, so consider how you will use the power of your voice. Many people are thirsty for affirmation and in need of help in the midst of despair. There are many people in your community, and around the world, who never hear kind things said to them or about them. There are people who know you but don't know Jesus. At times, you may use your voice to put others down or get a laugh. But how much greater would it be for you to use the power of your tongue to build up others? Use your voice to say, "Great job!" or "You're a good friend!" or "How can I pray for you?" You'll never be sorry you did!

1. *What is something your mom or dad has said to you that really meant a lot to you?*

_____

_____

_____

2. *What have you said that you wish you had not?*

_____

_____

_____

3. *What is something that someone has said to you that meant a lot to you, and how could you do that for someone else?*

_____

_____

_____

Read Ephesians 4:29.

4. *What does Ephesians say we should use our voice for, and how does that relate to Proverbs 18:21?*

_____

_____

_____

5. *After reading these two passages, write out three questions you have about these verses.*

1. _____

_____

_____

_____

2. _____

_____

_____

3. _____

_____

_____

6. *What other verses in the Bible help to answer your questions?*

_____

_____

_____

_____

7. *What do you think is the most important idea of these two passages, Ephesians 4:29 and Proverbs 18:21?*

_____

_____

_____

8. *What do these verses ask you to think, feel, or do?*

_____

_____

_____

_____

_____

WEEK 4

– TRUTH –

WHAT'S TRUE?

GETTING THE PROOF

> *Every word of God proves true;*
> *he is a shield to those who take refuge in him.*
>
> PROVERBS 30:5

When I was really young, my older brother did something wrong and was hoping I would take the blame. He carved my first name into a piece of furniture. Unfortunately for him, my parents had evidence of my innocence. I was so little at the time that I couldn't spell my name yet. Oops! My own inability to read and write was the proof I needed that my brother was to blame.

If you want to establish that something is true, you need evidence. We call that proof. How do you prove that a chair can hold up your weight? You sit on it. The proof that God's Word is true is that it has and can be proven. How do we know God loves us like He says in His Word? Jesus dying for us is our proof. How do we know that God's Word is true? God proves it is true by predicting things before they happen. Only God could do that. It could not be made up. How do we know that the proverbs you study in this book will be helpful? Try them out! Try to prove them! Living out the proverbs will lead you to a God who gave them to you so He could protect you and be your shield.

Sure, you'll find that proverbs are not promises. In other words, you'll find that God's proverbs are not a formula for getting what you want. The proverbs are principles. Principles are values and beliefs that drive our actions and choices. Proverbs are a guide to doing what is best. And they were given to you by God who knows what is best.

1. Where have you seen proof that God's Word is wisdom in the way your mom or dad lives out their faith?

_____

_____

_____

2. Have you ever felt like you had to prove that what you believed was true? How did you do it? What was your evidence?

_____

_____

_____

3. If God's Word says something, but you disagree, who do you think is right—you or God? How can you know?

_____

_____

_____

Read 2 Timothy 3:16–17.

4. Compare the uses for God's Word in Proverbs 30:5 and 2 Timothy 3:16–17. Based on these verses, how should we use the Bible?

_____

_____

_____

5. After reading these two passages, write out three questions you have about these texts.

    1. _____

_____

_____

_____

2. _____

_____

_____

_____

3. _____

_____

_____

_____

6. *What other verses in the Bible help to answer your questions?*

_____

_____

_____

_____

7. *What do you think is the most important idea of these two passages,*
2 Timothy 3:16–17 and Proverbs 30:5?

_____

_____

_____

8. *What do these verses ask or inspire you to think, feel, or do?*

_____

_____

_____

_____

_____

DON'T BELIEVE EVERYTHING YOU HEAR

> *The simple believes everything,*
> *but the prudent gives thought to his steps.*
>
> PROVERBS 14:15

When I was growing up, a bunch of my friends were into watching professional wrestling. That's when muscle-bound men in costumes perform wrestling stunts in a boxing ring. I didn't watch it, but my dad and my older brother swore to me it was fake, while my friends were convinced it was real. Who could I believe when the people I was closest to disagreed with one another?

As you grow up, you're going to be presented with a lot of different ideas. You will meet people from all sorts of religions and backgrounds. You will be taught different scientific theories, and you'll hear different political interpretations of the same events. How will you know who to believe?

The good news is that God gave you His Word, the Bible, to address your questions. He also blesses you with His people, the church, to walk with you. God calls you to be thoughtful about your steps instead of just assuming that everyone is telling you the truth. God's Word and Christ's life are the standard by which we judge whether the world is telling the truth. You can rely on what God says.

1. What is great about having a parent or godly adult that you can trust with your questions?

_____

_____

_____

2. Can you think of a time when someone told you something they believed that you did not?

_____

_____

_____

3. How will the Bible help you when you face difficult questions in life?

_____

_____

_____

Read Ephesians 5:6–10.

4. Why might someone want to deceive you, and how does Proverbs 14:15 help you not be fooled?

_____

_____

_____

5. After reading these two passages, write out three questions you have about these verses.

1. _____

_____

_____

2. _____

_____

_____

3. _____

_____

_____

6. What other verses in the Bible help to answer your questions?

_____

_____

_____

_____

7. What do you think is the most important idea of these two passages, Ephesians 5:6–10 and Proverbs 14:15?

_____

_____

_____

8. What do these verses ask you to think, feel, or do?

_____

_____

_____

_____

_____

GOD HAS A PLAN
AND YOU ARE PART OF IT

> *Many are the plans in a person's heart,*
> *but it is the Lord's purpose that prevails.*
>
> PROVERBS 19:21 NIV

I was on a basketball team that only had one good player. Guess what? It wasn't me. Our game plan in every game was pretty simple: if the ball comes to you, pass it to the good player. If for any reason he passes the ball to you, it's an easy fix—just pass it right back to him. This plan worked. The better we followed it, the better our team did.

We have a lot of plans, a lot of things we want to do that we think will bring us success or pleasure. You can have a lot of plans for your life, but in the end, it's only God's plan for your life that matters. God's plan is the one that will win, and it may be different than the plan you hoped for. That's okay. God can be trusted, so His plan is always going to be better than any plan we could come up with.

Since God is always good and always in charge, we can trust that His plan is good. This is true even when our life really, really hurts. God can still be trusted. After Joseph was betrayed by his brothers, sold into slavery, and eventually sent away to prison for a crime he did not commit, he still testified to God's good plan as he forgave his brothers and said to them, "You meant evil against me, but God meant it for good" (Genesis 50:20).

The good news is that God has a purpose for you in His plan. He made you like you are, where you are, and how you are to be part of what

He is accomplishing. He wrote your story out of love. You are the only "you" in God's plan. Praise God!

1. What kinds of good plans do you see your mom or dad make for your family?

_____

_____

_____

2. How can you use the unique mix of talents and gifts God gave you to serve God?

_____

_____

_____

3. What do you hope God's plan is for your future?

_____

_____

_____

Read Romans 8:28.

4. How do Romans 8:28 and Proverbs 19:21 shape the way you look at your hardest times?

_____

_____

_____

5. After reading these two passages, write out three questions you have about these verses.

1. _____

_____

_____

2. _____

_____

_____

3. _____

_____

_____

6. *What other verses in the Bible help to answer your questions?*

_____

_____

_____

_____

7. *What do you think is the most important idea of these two passages, Romans 8:28 and Proverbs 19:21?*

_____

_____

_____

8. *What do these verses ask you to think, feel, or do?*

_____

_____

_____

_____

_____

GUARDING YOUR HEART

> *Keep your heart with all vigilance,*
> *for from it flow the springs of life.*
>
> PROVERBS 4:23

Have you ever built a fort? Any old board or rusty nail can become an essential part of the fortress. When I built forts as a kid with my friends, other neighborhood kids would always come along and want to use what we built. We made sure to protect the pile of splintered garbage that was rightfully ours! We would collect big berries from nearby shrubs as ammunition, and we would happily hurl them in attempts to scare off any potential invaders.

Think of your mind and heart like a fort or a fortress. A lot of things can try to invade your mind and heart. Some of them may even seem innocent or desirable, but trust me, you don't want to let them in. Images that should be private for someone else or depictions of violence. Words that are mocking, filthy, or abusive. Thoughts that are deceptive, cruel, or mean. Like a guard at the gates of a fortress, keep them out of your mind and heart.

The Bible warns us to guard our hearts. Your God is wise enough to know that if you let an enemy in the gates, it can wreak havoc on your life. If you are worried about what you've already let into your mind, remember that God is forgiving, and He can make all things new. Join the psalmist in saying, "Create in me a clean heart, O God, and renew a right spirit within me" (Psalm 51:10).

1. When have you seen your mom or dad protecting you from something they didn't want you to see?

_____

_____

_____

2. What do you think it would take to avoid letting negative and evil things linger in your heart and mind?

_____

_____

_____

3. Why do you think God warns us to guard our hearts?

_____

_____

_____

Read Philippians 4:8.

4. One of these verses is about keeping things out of our mind and one is about letting certain things in. How are Proverbs 4:23 and Philippians 4:8 related?

_____

_____

_____

5. After reading these two passages, write out three questions you have about these verses.

    1. _____

       _____

       _____

2. _____

_____

_____

3. _____

_____

_____

6. What other verses in the Bible help to answer your questions?

_____

_____

_____

_____

7. What do you think is the most important idea of these two passages, Philippians 4:8 and Proverbs 4:23?

_____

_____

_____

8. What do these verses ask you to think, feel, or do?

_____

_____

_____

_____

_____

LISTENING TO GOOD ADVICE

> *Listen to advice and accept instruction,*
> *that you may gain wisdom in the future.*
>
> PROVERBS 19:20

Have you ever had lessons in playing an instrument? When I was growing up, I took guitar lessons. Every week my instructor would assign me homework and say, "The only way you're going to get any better is to practice." I can testify that he was right. I hated to practice. So, I never got better.

If you want to grow in wisdom, one of the best things you can do is believe and trust the advice you get from those who are wise. Experience and practice can also build wisdom. When you don't have any experience and you haven't had any practice, you can't expect to be very good. Practicing wisdom looks like trusting what God says and putting it into practice. This could mean doing things like repenting when you know you've done something wrong, returning something you stole, or being honest even when you're tempted to lie.

There are many situations you'll face in which you need to make a decision. You may even think you know what to choose. Be warned, though: where your choice is between what you desire to do and a godly thing you should do, don't just go with your gut. When what you want and what God says are two different things, please trust the voice of experience offered to you from godly parents, your church, and especially God in His Word. Let God be the loudest voice in your life. God will always be your best guide.

1. What is the best advice that your parents ever gave you?

_____

_____

_____

2. How will you know the difference between wisdom and bad advice from someone?

_____

_____

_____

3. What is an area of your life that would benefit from more experience and practice as you grow up?

_____

_____

_____

Read Matthew 7:24–27.

4. According to Proverbs 19:20 and Matthew 7:24–27, what are some benefits to listening to wisdom from God?

_____

_____

_____

5. After reading these two passages, write out three questions you have about these verses.

1. _____

_____

_____

2. _____

   _____

   _____

3. _____

   _____

   _____

6. *What other verses in the Bible help to answer your questions?*

_____

_____

_____

_____

7. *What do you think is the most important idea of these two passages, Matthew 7:24–27 and Proverbs 19:20?*

_____

_____

_____

8. *What do these verses ask you to think, feel, or do?*

_____

_____

_____

_____

WEEK 5

—IDENTITY—

WHO AM I?

WHAT ARE YOU KNOWN FOR?

A good name is to be chosen rather than great riches,
and favor is better than silver or gold.

PROVERBS 22:1

I was a very, very poorly behaved elementary school kid. I didn't know how to sit still, and I didn't know how to be quiet. I even got into numerous physical fights. I gave a kid a bloody nose for cutting in front of me in line and broke another kid's arm for making fun of me on the bus. In short, I was a troublemaker. I attended the same small school in the same small town for eight years, so it didn't take long for my lack of self-control to become notorious among the school's faculty. Whether it's deserved or not, once you get a reputation, it can be hard to shake it. After a few years, teachers assumed any trouble in their classroom was probably my fault even if it wasn't.

While God has warned us against the dangers of seeking the approval of others, He also speaks to the value of having a "good name" and "favor" as a result of godly character. In fact, Jesus says that when you are obedient to Him, you get the privilege of demonstrating the character of God to others. Your God-glorifying reputation is built on what other people see of your actions, words, and moods.

The good news for those who follow Jesus is that every one of our personality flaws and shortcomings can be forgiven and transformed in Christ. Who you were yesterday does not determine who you are today. I'm not doomed to be a "troublemaker." I'm a changed man, and my reputation is built on who I am in Christ. Since God's mercies are new every morning, every day is a new chance to pursue the kind of godly integrity that glorifies God and leads to being known for humility, kindness, and joy.

1. *What are a few positive words you would use to describe your mom or dad's personality?*

_____

_____

_____

_____

2. *How would the people who know you best describe you? What is your reputation?*

_____

_____

_____

_____

3. *What do you wish you were known for?*

_____

_____

_____

_____

Read Matthew 5:16.

4. *How does having a good name, like in Proverbs 22:1, bring glory to God like it calls us to in Matthew 5:16?*

_____

_____

_____

_____

5. After reading these two passages, write out three questions you have about these verses.

1. _____

_____

_____

2. _____

_____

_____

3. _____

_____

_____

6. What other verses in the Bible help to answer your questions?

_____

_____

_____

7. What do you think is the most important idea of these two passages, Matthew 5:16 and Proverbs 22:1?

_____

_____

_____

8. What do these verses ask you to think, feel, or do?

_____

_____

_____

THE NEED TO BE LIKED

> *The fear of man lays a snare,*
> *but whoever trusts in the LORD is safe.*
>
> PROVERBS 29:25

We care so much about what other people think about us. God says that it's a "snare" to spend your life seeking the approval of others in order to feel okay about yourself. A snare is a trap. It's something that looks good or seems safe, but stepping into it will capture and hurt you.

It's dangerous to live your life according to what will please other people. Others will have a way that seems right, but God tells us it's wrong, and the only way to please them will be to live according to that false way.

If, however, you trust in the Lord, if you live convinced that all the approval and love you want you already have in Christ, you will live safely. Not that you won't suffer. Following Jesus will lead to hardship, but you will be on a path to life and truth. God wants us to be wise enough not to fall for the trap of seeking approval at the expense of godliness. God already loves you, and He has made that obvious by giving His Son Jesus to die for you. Through His life, death, and resurrection eternal life with Him is guaranteed to everyone who trusts Him.

1. What is something that seems good that your mom or dad have warned you against?

_____

_____

2. Why is it dangerous to live only according to what other people think of you?

_____

_____

_____

3. How would you describe how God feels about you?

_____

_____

_____

Read Luke 12:4–7.

4. How does the fear talked about in Luke 12:4–7 differ from the fear in Proverbs 29:25?

_____

_____

_____

5. After reading these two passages, write out three questions you have about these verses.

1. _____

_____

_____

2. _____

_____

_____

3. _____

_____

_____

6. *What other verses in the Bible help to answer your questions?*

_____

_____

_____

_____

7. *What do you think is the most important idea of these two passages, Luke 12:4–7 and Proverbs 29:25?*

_____

_____

_____

8. *What do these verses ask you to think, feel, or do?*

_____

_____

_____

_____

_____

I WANT WHAT YOU HAVE

> *Fret not yourself because of evildoers,*
> *and be not envious of the wicked,*
> *for the evil man has no future;*
> *the lamp of the wicked will be put out.*
>
> PROVERBS 24:19–20

My family didn't have cool video games growing up. When all my friends at school were getting the newest game system with the best graphics, we were still playing an ancient technology they'd never heard about. I'd be lying if I said that I never thought about having what the other kids had. I was jealous.

This proverb tells us that there may come a time when you're tempted to envy or be jealous of someone getting something you wish you had. In fact, it is specifically warning us not to wish we had something that "evildoers" have. There will be a lot of people in your life who seem more successful than you even though they don't have integrity and humility. Don't envy them. Not only because earthly treasure is not worth building your life on, but because the way of wickedness and evil has no future.

Instead of envying those who gain success and material things while living godless lives, have pity and compassion on them. What they need is the same thing you need—Jesus.

1. *What is something your mom or dad have done for you that makes you feel grateful for your family?*

_____

_____

_____

2. *What is dangerous about envying someone who is godless?*

_____

_____

_____

3. *Why is Jesus better than anything else you could want?*

_____

_____

_____

Read James 3:16.

4. *Describe the kind of envy you see in both James 3:16 and Proverbs 24:19–20.*

_____

_____

_____

5. *After reading these two passages, write out three questions you have about these verses.*

1. _____

_____

_____

2. _____

_____

_____

3. _____

_____

_____

6. *What other verses in the Bible help to answer your questions?*

_____

_____

_____

_____

7. *What do you think is the most important idea of these two passages, James 3:16 and Proverbs 24:19–20?*

_____

_____

_____

8. *What do these verses ask you to think, feel, or do?*

_____

_____

_____

_____

_____

READY TO BE DIFFERENT

> *My son, do not walk in the way with them;*
> *hold back your foot from their paths.*
>
> PROVERBS 1:15

Do you know how to ride a bike? Going down a steep hill on a bike can be so much fun! Of course, to get to the top of it means having to bike uphill. Biking up a huge hill is tough and not nearly as fun as the effortless plunge back down.

In your life, there are going to be a lot of paths that are easier and some that are harder. It is almost always going to be easier to go along with whatever the people around you think is good and right. But if you are following Jesus, you need to be ready to face a lot of difficulty with other people your age. Following God will involve being ready to be different than many of the other kids at your school or in your neighborhood. It is a commitment to a harder and better path.

When you are different, people make fun of you. When you think differently, people get angry or offended. When you act or believe differently, you'll stick out for reasons that others might not like. Are you ready to be different? Christians must be resilient and strong. Never go with the crowd unless the crowd is following Jesus. Being liked may be the easier path to take, but it is often not leading you toward truth.

1. When do you remember your mom or dad being comfortable with being different?

_____

_____

_____

2. What makes being different difficult?

_____

_____

_____

3. Why should Christians be ready to be "unliked" and even ridiculed or persecuted for following God?

_____

_____

_____

Read Philippians 2:15.

4. How is sticking out like a "shining star" a good description for being different like someone who lives according to Proverbs 1:15?

_____

_____

_____

5. After reading these two passages, write out three questions you have about these verses.

    1. _____

_____

_____

2. _____

_____

_____

3. _____

_____

_____

6. *What other verses in the Bible help to answer your questions?*

_____

_____

_____

_____

7. *What do you think is the most important idea of these two passages,*
Philippians 2:15 and Proverbs 1:15?

_____

_____

_____

8. *What do these verses ask you to think, feel, or do?*

_____

_____

_____

_____

WHERE CAN YOU FIND YOUR VALUE?

> *Charm is deceptive, and beauty is fleeting;*
> *but a woman who fears the Lord is to be praised.*
>
> PROVERBS 31:30 NIV

Have you ever wished you could change something about the way you look? It's normal to want to change something about your physical appearance. Everyone has some desire to be admired, and everyone can find something they think would make them more attractive.

Whether it's the stars in the sky, a sunset over the ocean, mountains on the horizon, or the smile on the face of someone who loves you, God put beauty in the world as a gift to us. Our culture puts a lot of value on attractiveness and outward beauty. But your value doesn't fluctuate based on whether people think you are beautiful or charming.

When an adult meets someone they want to marry, they learn that beauty isn't as important as a person's faith, character, and person-ality. It's a great thing to find shared physical attraction in a romantic relationship, but someone loving God is infinitely more important than their shape on the outside.

Unlike people who don't believe in God, Christians value their faith in God above anything, and we value everyone no matter what they look like. Every person has value because God made them.

1. What trait do you think your mom and dad would say they like most about you?

_____

_____

_____

2. Why do you think our culture puts so much value on beauty?

_____

_____

_____

3. What do you think would be some important things to know about someone you might marry?

_____

_____

_____

Read 1 Peter 3:3–4.

4. What do 1 Peter 3:3–4 and Proverbs 31:30 say makes someone beautiful?

_____

_____

_____

5. After reading these two passages, write out three questions you have about these verses.

1. _____

_____

_____

2. _____

_____

_____

, 3. _____

_____

_____

6. What other verses in the Bible help to answer your questions?

.

_____

_____

_____

_____

7. What do you think is the most important idea of these two passages, 1 Peter 3:3–4 and Proverbs 31:30?

_____

_____

_____

8. What do these verses ask you to think, feel, or do?

_____

_____

_____

_____

_____

WEEK 6

—RELATIONSHIPS—

WHAT ABOUT

OTHER PEOPLE?

FRIENDSHIP

> *Make no friendship with a man given to anger,*
> *nor go with a wrathful man,*
> *lest you learn his ways*
> *and entangle yourself in a snare.*
>
> PROVERBS 22:24–25

Some of the most important choices you will ever make in your entire life are who your friends will be and what kind of friend you will be. Are your friends building you up or tearing you down? Are you leading or being led . . . and in what direction? It was from friends that I learned words that should never be said. It was because my friends were going that I have gone places I was not supposed to go. It was because my friends were doing them that I tried substances and activities that should never be tried.

I have had many friends that were "bad influences." If I'm being totally honest, many times I have been a friend that was a bad influence on others too. I have both followed friends away from God, and I have led friends away from God's wisdom. That's being a bad influence. Sin can start with what seems like innocent fun with friends, but Proverbs calls it a snare—a trap you don't see coming.

The Bible warns us about making friendships with people who will teach us or lead us into foolishness instead of wisdom. That doesn't mean that you should only be friends with Christians, nor does it mean that Christians should look down on others. What it *does* mean is that you should be wise about who you spend time around because they will have a big impact on your life.

If you find that one of your friendships is leading you to rebel against God, then that friendship is not worth it. It is great to share your faith with a friend who needs Jesus, but you should never go along with sin just to maintain a friendship. A true friend respects your choices even if in wisdom you differ from them. Be a leader in your friendships.

1. What are traits you see in your mom or dad that you would love to find in a good friend?

_____

_____

_____

2. What do you think it means "lest you learn his ways"?

_____

_____

_____

3. What are qualities you look for in a good friendship?

_____

_____

_____

Read John 15:13–15.

4. In John 15, Jesus says that friendship with Him is related to obedience. Proverbs 22:24–25 warns us about what kind of friends to avoid. Based on these two verses, list things you do and don't want in a friend.

_____

_____

_____

5. After reading these two passages, write out three questions you have about these verses.

1. _____

_____

_____

2. _____

_____

_____

3. _____

_____

_____

6. What other verses in the Bible help to answer your questions?

_____

_____

_____

7. What do you think is the most important idea of these two passages, John 15:13–15 and Proverbs 22:24–25?

_____

_____

_____

8. What do these verses ask you to think, feel, or do?

_____

_____

_____

TIME TO IMPROVE

> *Iron sharpens iron,*
> *and one man sharpens another.*
>
> PROVERBS 27:17

In my family, there are a lot of competitions that I lose regularly, but not when it comes to ping-pong. I am used to winning at ping-pong. Here's the problem, though: the more I play with my sons and my wife, the better they are getting. The day is coming soon when their skills will have caught up to mine, and I will have to relinquish my table tennis crown.

Proverbs 27:17 explains this principle. Being around smart, strong, and wise people can make you smarter, stronger, wiser, and better. There are a lot of ways that mentors, teachers, and coaches help us develop skills in things like music, sports, and classes. God calls you to be growing in your skills and in wisdom.

You probably know someone who is wiser than you, has overcome temptations in areas where you struggle, and has been following God longer. Spending time with them and talking about your life will help you gain wisdom and work through any challenges as you follow God. Think of someone you know and admire and consider what they are like. How do they handle their successes and their mistakes? Observing the way they live their life will be one of your best teachers.

1. How has your mom or dad (or another adult) helped you become wiser?

_____

_____

_____

2. As you follow God, what are some areas of your life that you would like to see improve?

_____

_____

_____

3. Who is someone in your life that is strong in that area, and how can you spend more time with them?

_____

_____

_____

Read 2 Corinthians 3:18.

4. Second Corinthians 3:18 talks about changing one degree at a time. How could you combine Proverbs 27:17 and this verse from 2 Corinthians into one statement?

_____

_____

_____

5. After reading these two passages, write out three questions you have about these verses.

1. _____

_____

_____

2. _____

_____

_____

3. _____

_____

_____

6. What other verses in the Bible help to answer your questions?

_____

_____

_____

_____

7. What do you think is the most important idea of these two passages, 2 Corinthians 3:18 and Proverbs 27:17?

_____

_____

_____

8. What do these verses ask you to think, feel, or do?

_____

_____

_____

_____

_____

THE GREAT THING ABOUT PARENTS

> *Listen, my son, to your father's instruction*
> *and do not forsake your mother's teaching.*
>
> PROVERBS 1:8 NIV

I can't think of a harder job on the entire planet than being a parent. I know for a fact it was hard to be my parent. I personally made sure that my mom and dad faced a significant challenge. I complained when something wasn't exactly how I wanted it. I threw a fit and lost my temper when things didn't go my way. I blamed my parents for my problems. I constantly thought about what my mom and dad should be doing for me, and I never thought about what might be a blessing to them. I did things they told me not to do, and sometimes, I did it on purpose. When I was a kid, I chose to be rude, selfish, thoughtless, and disrespectful.

While your parents aren't perfect, it's not your job, as a son or daughter, to be their boss. You are to learn from them, obey them, and honor them. God gave fathers and mothers an important and challenging assignment: caring for and leading their children. It takes a lot for an imperfect man or woman to do that well. Today would be a good day to extend your parents grace for their shortcomings and love for all their best efforts. God loves it when we show respect and appreciation to our parents. God gave them a hard job. Make their job a little easier by trusting their godly wisdom.

Proverbs 1:8 reminds us of all the good things that our parents have told us. "Do not forsake" means that we should remain committed to those things we've learned from them. If you have parents who love Jesus and tell you about Him, listen to them and be grateful for any of the wisdom they have to offer you!

1. What is a creative way that you could show your mom or dad that you love them today?

_____

_____

_____

2. Where do you see your mom or dad struggling in a way that you could pray for them or talk with them about?

_____

_____

_____

3. What would change in your home if you started to honor your parents in all things?

_____

_____

_____

Read Ephesians 6:1–3.

4. What do Ephesians 6:1–3 and Proverbs 1:8 tell us about how God wants us to treat our parents?

_____

_____

_____

5. After reading these two passages, write out three questions you have about these texts.

1. _____
   _____
   _____

2. _____
   _____
   _____

3. _____
   _____
   _____

6. What other verses in the Bible help to answer your questions?

_____
_____
_____

7. What do you think is the most important idea of these two passages, Ephesians 6:1–3 and Proverbs 1:8?

_____
_____
_____

8. What do these verses ask you to think, feel, or do?

_____
_____
_____

PATIENCE OR VENGEANCE

> *Good sense makes one slow to anger,*
> *and it is his glory to overlook an offense.*
>
> PROVERBS 19:11

I used to get in a lot of fights at school when I was a kid. If someone hit me, I almost always hit them back. If I started it, if I hit first, someone almost always swung back at me. In all the fights I've ever been in, I cannot remember a single one that solved a problem. In other words, hitting someone never made my problems better. Losing my temper never gave me what I truly wanted.

In God's wisdom, He teaches us that forgiveness is *always* better than revenge. Retribution, or getting someone back for what they did to you, is never godly. We are all hurt sometimes by what other people do to us. Many of those hurts should be addressed with a trusted friend or adult who can come alongside you and help you where you've been harmed, but retaliation will never be an acceptable justification for acting poorly.

While the world may justify "getting someone back," those of us who follow God know that it's always better to remain coolheaded and forgive an offense whenever we can.

1. When have you seen your mom or dad be patient?

_____

_____

_____

2. Why do you think we are tempted to hurt people who hurt us?

_____

_____

_____

3. What calms you down when you are angry?

_____

_____

_____

Read Ephesians 4:1–3.

4. What do you think "bearing with one another" has to do with Proverbs 19:11?

_____

_____

_____

5. After reading these two passages, write out three questions you have about these verses.

1. _____

_____

_____

2. _____

_____

_____

3. _____

_____

_____

6. *What other verses in the Bible help to answer your questions?*

_____

_____

_____

_____

7. *What do you think is the most important idea of these two passages, Ephesians 4:1–3 and Proverbs 19:11?*

_____

_____

_____

8. *What do these verses ask you to think, feel, or do?*

_____

_____

_____

_____

_____

GIVING IS GREAT

> *One person gives freely, yet gains even more;*
> *another withholds unduly, but comes to poverty.*
> *A generous person will prosper;*
> *whoever refreshes others will be refreshed.*
>
> PROVERBS 11:24–25 NIV

When I was growing up, my parents had me put 50 percent of every dollar I got into a savings account. Every dollar. Not just from paychecks once I had a job, I'm talking about money in my birthday cards from Grandma. In addition, they had me set aside 10 percent to be given to our local church. They were teaching me a really important lesson. First, they taught me to spend what I had responsibly. Second, they taught me that 100 percent of everything I had belonged to God. So, together with our fellow church members, we offer some of what we earn to accomplish God's mission in our community. Being generous with what we have is a way of worshiping and a way of blessing others.

Being generous isn't just good for us because it feels good to bless others; giving reminds us of the truth that the money God has given us isn't just for us to hold on to or spend on ourselves.

Now, as an adult, I still try to save and spend responsibly, and my wife and I set aside money so we can be generous to others. Our friends who don't follow Jesus are confused about why we'd "give away" much of what we've earned. What they don't understand is that everything we've been entrusted with is God's anyway, so we trust Him to tell us what to do with it. God is a generous God, and He loves it when we are generous too.

1. When have you seen your mom or dad be truly generous to you or others?

_____

_____

_____

2. Why is it hard to be generous sometimes?

_____

_____

_____

3. What do you have right now that would be a blessing to someone else if you gave it to them?

_____

_____

_____

Read 2 Corinthians 9:6–7.

4. Now that you read 2 Corinthians 9:6–7 and Proverbs 11:24–25, how do you think we should feel when we genuinely want to bless others with what we have?

_____

_____

_____

_____

5. After reading these two passages, write out three questions you have about these verses.

1. _____
_____
_____

2. _____
_____
_____

3. _____
_____
_____

6. What other verses in the Bible help to answer your questions?

_____
_____
_____

7. What do you think is the most important idea of these two passages, 2 Corinthians 9:6–7 and Proverbs 11:24–25?

_____
_____
_____

8. What do these verses ask you to think, feel, or do?

_____
_____
_____

WEEK 7

— STRUGGLES —

WHAT ABOUT SIN?

YOUR SIN SENSE

> *There are those who are clean in their own eyes*
> *but are not washed of their filth.*
>
> PROVERBS 30:12

If you've been around a particular smell long enough, you can develop "nose blindness." Nose blindness is when you stop noticing a smell you've gotten used to. For example, if you're sweaty and stinky and you have been for some time, friends nearby might encounter a strong stench that you can't detect because you've gotten used to it.

God says that there are people—and sometimes you are one of them—who aren't good at noticing their own sin and failings. Sin thrives in our blind spots. Whether it's because you think you are better than the people around you or because you are ignorant of what God calls sin, it's easy to overlook your own flaws. Or maybe you don't address your sin on purpose because you like how that sin makes you feel or because you disagree with what God defines as wrong. In those cases, look to the Bible as your authority on what is right since God is the author and creator of life.

The danger of not noticing or recognizing our sin is that we would continue to disobey God without struggling against it. God warns us against sin for a reason. Obedience to God actually brings us great joy while sin causes harm to us and others. On the bright side, if you get help from others and the Word of God, you can be washed clean of sin—and, thanks to the grace of God, even see victory over it. Wouldn't it be great to find freedom from sin? We won't have to deal with sin in heaven, but it's so kind of God to help us overcome here and now. Putting sin behind us is always a blessing!

1. How do you respond to your parents when you know they are right about something you're doing wrong?

_____

_____

_____

2. What are sins you see in yourself and others that you think are hard to detect or defeat?

_____

_____

_____

3. Why should Christians want to put sin "to death" in their lives?

_____

_____

_____

Read Luke 18:9–14.

4. How does Proverbs 30:12 apply to the two men in this parable that Jesus told?

_____

_____

_____

5. After reading these two passages, write out three questions you have about these verses.

1. _____

_____

_____

2. _____

_____

_____

3. _____

_____

_____

6. *What other verses in the Bible help to answer your questions?*

_____

_____

_____

_____

7. *What do you think is the most important idea of these two passages, Luke 18:9–14 and Proverbs 30:12?*

_____

_____

_____

8. *What do these verses ask you to think, feel, or do?*

_____

_____

_____

_____

_____

GOD CARES ABOUT
WHAT YOU EAT AND DRINK

> *Wine is a mocker and beer a brawler;*
> *whoever is led astray by them is not wise.*
>
> PROVERBS 20:1

I remember when my friends at school started to smoke cigarettes and drink alcohol. It felt fun to do something that was forbidden. If your friends start to smoke, drink, or do drugs, you might start to feel pressure from them to join in. God has something better for you.

Drugs and alcohol affect the way you feel, think, and act. Some people use substances to numb their bad feelings or escape their problems. Many of these substances change our ability to think clearly, and they stop people from making good decisions. Some people develop addictions to drugs or alcohol. That means they come to depend on these substances to function, and they may not be able to stop depending on them.

God actually warns us about the kind of choices we make when we sacrifice good judgment for drinking alcohol or taking drugs. Being "led astray" by a substance is foolish. There is wisdom and great joy in being sober and being free of addiction. Because God cares about you, He cares about what you put into your body.

1. What kinds of healthy things do your parents like to eat and drink, or what healthy habits do you see in your family?

_____

_____

2. Why do you think God warns us about abusing drugs and alcohol?

_____

_____

3. Why does God care about what we eat or drink, or whether we smoke?

_____

_____

_____

Read Ephesians 5:18.

4. What alternative does Ephesians 5:18 offer to drunkenness or being led astray by wine and beer as in Proverbs 20:1?

_____

_____

_____

5. After reading these two passages, write out three questions you have about these verses.

1. _____

_____

_____

2. _____

   _____

   _____

3. _____

   _____

   _____

6. What other verses in the Bible help to answer your questions?

_____

_____

_____

_____

7. What do you think is the most important idea of these two passages, Ephesians 5:18 and Proverbs 20:1?

_____

_____

_____

8. What do these verses ask you to think, feel, or do?

_____

_____

_____

_____

BOTH DESIRABLE AND DESTRUCTIVE

> *Can a man carry fire next to his chest*
> *and his clothes not be burned?*
>
> PROVERBS 6:27

When I was a boy, I wondered how girls' bodies were different than mine. I would try to look things up in dictionaries and encyclopedias to solve the mystery. Pursuing that kind of curiosity about other people's bodies can easily lead to seeing or reading or watching things that can hurt our hearts and minds . . . and even lead us away from God.

There are a lot of images and videos and even relationships in the world that are both desirable and destructive. It is a common temptation to want to chase the things we desire in a way that will turn other people into objects that only exist to please our senses. Being tempted by sinful physical desires and attractions is called lust. Giving in to these sinful feelings can seem good because it may feel good in the moment. But there is a reason God warned us against lust, even in our own thoughts. This proverb reminds us that you can't interact with something destructive and come away unharmed.

God loves you, and He is for your good. Your feelings can have a godly purpose. You are intended for one long-term relationship with someone of the opposite sex within the covenant of marriage . . . or for a life of beautiful, contented singleness. Instead of sin, the Bible tells us to chase after righteousness, faith, and the love of God.

1. Ask your parents what godly qualities they think are important in a spouse.

_____

_____

_____

2. Why do you think lust is a difficult sin for some people to talk about?

_____

_____

_____

3. When you are struggling with desires to do things you know you shouldn't, who will you talk to?

_____

_____

_____

Read 1 Corinthians 6:18.

4. What should be our approach to sexual sin according to 1 Corinthians 6:18? How does the warning of Proverbs 6:27 help us understand why God might advise us to flee?

_____

_____

_____

5. After reading these two passages, write out three questions you have about these verses.

1. _____

_____

_____

2. _____

_____

_____

3. _____

_____

_____

6. *What other verses in the Bible help to answer your questions?*

_____

_____

_____

_____

7. *What do you think is the most important idea of these two passages,*
1 Corinthians 6:18 and Proverbs 6:27?

_____

_____

_____

8. *What do these verses ask you to think, feel, or do?*

_____

_____

_____

_____

_____

AVOIDING DANGER

> *The prudent sees danger and hides himself,*
> *but the simple go on and suffer for it.*
>
> PROVERBS 27:12

My family and I went on a drive-thru safari once. We could feed all kinds of animals right out of our car windows and giraffes through our minivan sunroof! The park warns you about the ostrich, though. To feed it, you should throw the food on the ground. DO NOT hold the feed pellets in your hand. Did I hear this warning? Yes. Did I still feed the ostrich out of my hand? Yes. Did the ostrich bite my pinky finger so hard that I thought I'd never see it again? Yes. Was what I did foolish and dangerous? Absolutely!

Proverbs warns us that if you see danger, don't be so foolish as to walk into it anyway. One of the dangers you will face most often will be the temptation to sin, the desire to disobey God. No matter how many times you are warned, you may still want to do something that you know you shouldn't. The wise person refuses to indulge their temptations. But the "simple" (foolish) person just goes with their sinful gut and pays the price.

God has warned you against sin, not because He hates fun, but because He loves you. He can be trusted. When you feel tempted to go in a direction He's warned you against, please be wise instead of foolish. And when you do mess up, confess it and rely on the grace of God to forgive you.

1. What is a good rule in your home that you've been tempted to break?

_____

_____

_____

2. Why do you think sin can be so tempting?

_____

_____

_____

3. What will it take for you to choose to follow God even when disobedience seems more fun?

_____

_____

_____

Read James 1:14–15.

4. What kind of warnings do you see in both James 1:14–15 and Proverbs 27:12?

_____

_____

_____

5. After reading these two passages, write out three questions you have about these verses.

    1. _____

    _____

    _____

2. _____

_____

_____

3. _____

_____

_____

6. *What other verses in the Bible help to answer your questions?*

_____

_____

_____

_____

7. *What do you think is the most important idea of these two passages, James 1:14–15 and Proverbs 27:12?*

_____

_____

_____

8. *What do these verses ask you to think, feel, or do?*

_____

_____

_____

_____

_____

TIME TO QUIT

> *Whoever conceals his transgressions will not prosper, but he who confesses and forsakes them will obtain mercy.*
>
> PROVERBS 28:13

I remember playing hide and seek with a friend when I was a kid. I had hidden for so long in the woods without being found that I eventually quit and walked back home. When I got there, I found out that my friend had been picked up by his mom an hour before. Embarrassing. Imagine if I had never quit. I might still be out there!

Quitting isn't always bad. Sure, we shouldn't give up on something good just because it's hard, but we want to quit the things in life that are harmful, unkind, or mistakes. We want to quit being mean to people. We want to quit lying. We want to quit choosing ourselves over others.

In Proverbs 28:13, "transgressions" is a big word for sin, or the ways we don't follow God. The word "forsake" means to quit. This proverb is about not hiding your sin and not continuing in it; it's about quitting sin. The verse also reminds us that there is compassion, love, and forgiveness for sinners in the heart of God. You don't need to hide your mistakes from God who loves you so much! Tell your parents and friends about your struggles, mistakes, and temptations.

Most importantly, share them with God in prayer, and you'll be surprised how much kindness God will show you despite your imperfections. There's a reason God wants us to quit sin: it is destructive. When you notice yourself doing, saying, or thinking things that don't honor God—confess them, quit them, and enjoy God's grace for you.

1. Can you think of a time when your parents had mercy on you when you confessed some of your mistakes?

_____

_____

_____

2. What is something you do that you want to stop doing because you know it does not honor God?

_____

_____

_____

3. What is something you want to start doing because you think it would honor God?

_____

_____

_____

Read 1 John 1:8–10.

4. What is the good news about our sin that 1 John 1:8–10 and Proverbs 28:13 show us?

_____

_____

_____

5. *After reading these two passages, write out three questions you have about these verses.*

1. _____

   _____

   _____

2. _____

   _____

   _____

3. _____

   _____

   _____

6. What other verses in the Bible help to answer your questions?

_____

_____

_____

7. What do you think is the most important idea of these two passages, 1 John 1:8–10 and Proverbs 28:13?

_____

_____

_____

8. What do these verses ask you to think, feel, or do?

_____

_____

_____

WEEK 8

— PERSEVERANCE —

WHAT NOW?

HARD WORK

> *In all toil there is profit,*
> *but mere talk tends only to poverty.*
>
> PROVERBS 14:23

In high school, I had a job at an ice cream and burger restaurant. The place was always busy, mostly because our food was super good. The other servers and I would get worn out scooping banana splits, mixing shakes, and flipping burgers. I'd always go home with sore feet. If serving customers ever did slow down for a minute, my coworkers and I would lean against a wall or a counter for a break and conversation. Of course, if our manager saw us, she'd yell out, "If you've got time to lean, you've got time to clean!" and we'd hop to doing dishes, wiping counters, and mopping the floor. The work never stopped. It was hard, but I loved that job.

God made you to do hard things, to face challenges and overcome them. God is not a mean boss; He is a loving Father who has high expectations for His children whom He loves. The calling on your life, the work God has for you, is not always easy, but that's what's so great about being a Christian. The God who has given you the hard task of struggling against sin and pursuing righteousness is also the God who empowers you for it, does it with you, and forgives you when you fall short.

Followers of Christ are people who toil. That means they work hard. When we are asked to do something, we give it our best without grumbling. We expect to struggle, but we expect toil to make us stronger and overcoming challenges to bring glory to God.

1. When have you seen your family work hard and not give up?

_____

_____

_____

2. What do you think it means that "in all toil there is profit"?

_____

_____

_____

3. What would following God look like if it was "mere talk"?

_____

_____

_____

Read Colossians 3:23–24.

4. What kind of person do you imagine when you read Colossians 3:23–24 and Proverbs 14:23? What are they doing?

_____

_____

_____

5. After reading these two passages, write out three questions you have about these verses.

1. _____

_____

_____

2. _____

_____

_____

3. _____

_____

_____

6. *What other verses in the Bible help to answer your questions?*

_____

_____

_____

_____

7. *What do you think is the most important idea of these two passages,*
Colossians 3:23–24 and Proverbs 14:23?

_____

_____

_____

8. *What do these verses ask you to think, feel, or do?*

_____

_____

_____

_____

RESILIENCE

> *For the righteous falls seven times and rises again,*
> *but the wicked stumble in times of calamity.*
>
> PROVERBS 24:16

In our house, we've had an ant problem in our kitchen so many times that I've almost given up and just invited the queen to move into our guest room. No matter how many entrances we plug up or how often exterminators spray ant repellents around our house, the ants always find a new way in. They won't give up. They just keep coming.

Proverbs 24:16 tells us that those who follow God just keep coming. They are relentless. When it comes to following God in your generation, you are going to have to be resilient because you will face a lot of opposition. In those moments of difficulty, when it feels like your reputation is at risk or you feel unwanted, embarrassed, or just discouraged, consider the resilience God has called you to.

When you are walking in godliness, you can have confidence about your choices. Don't give up on your efforts to do what's right. God has given His people the strength we need to persevere even through suffering for the sake of serving Him. Never give up on following Jesus, but don't be surprised when it gets hard and requires resilience.

1. What is something hard that your mom or dad has to keep doing in order to serve your family?

_____

_____

_____

2. When was a time that you faced opposition and refused to give in?

_____

_____

_____

3. How will you follow God when the people around you do not?

_____

_____

_____

Read James 1:12.

4. What does James 1:12 say you will receive if you don't give up? How is that related to Proverbs 24:16?

_____

_____

_____

5. After reading these two passages, write out three questions you have about these verses.

1. _____

_____

_____

2. _____

_____

_____

3. _____

_____

_____

6. What other verses in the Bible help to answer your questions?

_____

_____

_____

_____

7. What do you think is the most important idea of these two passages, James 1:12 and Proverbs 24:16?

_____

_____

_____

8. What do these verses ask you to think, feel, or do?

_____

_____

_____

_____

_____

NO MORE EXCUSES

> *The sluggard says, "There is a lion outside!*
> *I shall be killed in the streets!"*
>
> PROVERBS 22:13

A "sluggard" is a lazy person, someone who does not want to do their work. When we don't want to do something, it's not hard to come up with a reason not to do it. This proverb is a warning about making excuses.

Can you imagine telling your parents that you didn't take out the garbage because there was a lion waiting outside your house? Do you think you'd get away with it? Is there any chore you could skip because you feared a dangerous wild animal might attack you? "I can't wash the dishes! There could be an alligator in the drain!"

This proverb is exaggerating how ridiculous excuses can get when we try to find a way out of doing what we are supposed to. The sad truth is we often don't do the things we know are right simply because we don't want to. It's not because we are incapable or uninformed. If we're honest, we know what we should do, but we justify not doing it. When there is pressure to conform to an ungodly crowd or behavior, we will be tempted to make excuses about sin. Just because some sin is common, or because it seems victimless, or because you think it's not a big deal, is no excuse to choose sin over God. Just because what you're called to do or be seems hard, or embarrassing, or unattainable, is no excuse for not pursuing righteousness. Sin may seem right, but in the end, it leads to death.

1. What are things you know your parents want to see you do or be that you typically resist?

_____

_____

_____

2. What excuses do you find yourself making for doing things you shouldn't or neglecting to do what you should?

_____

_____

_____

3. Why do you think we make excuses?

_____

_____

_____

Read Luke 9:59–62.

4. How does Proverbs 22:13 relate to the excuses potential disciples are making in Luke 9:59–62? How does Jesus respond to excuses?

_____

_____

_____

5. After reading these two passages, write out three questions you have about these verses.

1. _____

_____

_____

2. _____

_____

_____

3. _____

_____

_____

6. What other verses in the Bible help to answer your questions?

_____

_____

_____

_____

7. What do you think is the most important idea of these two passages, Luke 9:59–62 and Proverbs 22:13?

_____

_____

_____

8. What do these verses ask you to think, feel, or do?

_____

_____

_____

_____

_____

WITHOUT ANYONE TELLING YOU WHAT TO DO

*Go to the ant, O sluggard; consider
her ways, and be wise.
Without having any chief, officer,
or ruler, she prepares her bread in summer
and gathers her food in harvest.*

PROVERBS 6:6–8

Have you ever kicked an ant hill? The ants come pouring out of the natural disaster you just made of their home, and they immediately get to work rebuilding what was destroyed. They don't wait for orders or payment. They don't need bribes or threats. They don't look for instructions. They just get to work because that's what ants do. God says we could learn something from them. God tells us that it is wise to be ready to do what you're supposed to do even before someone asks you to do it. Like an ant who gathers food so that it has it when it needs it. And it does that without even being asked.

Do you only do work around your home when you are forced or convinced to do it? Do you ever try to get away with doing the bare minimum even when someone has asked you to do a lot more? Doing less will often feel like the better choice to us, but God wisely tells us that a life of ease and leisure is not our goal.

A godly man or woman does the right thing even when no one has asked or commanded them to. In fact, James tells us that if we know the right thing to do and don't do it, we are disobeying God. While God has so much grace for us when we mess up, He also has so much wisdom for how we should be striving to live. Let's be the kind of people who honor God by doing the right thing, doing it the best we can, and getting to it even before someone has to ask us to.

1. What is something you get asked to do around your house that would bless your parents if you started doing it without being asked?

_____

_____

_____

2. What is something you know you should do but you really try to avoid having to do it?

_____

_____

_____

3. Why do you think God cares about whether or not we do what's right?

_____

_____

_____

Read James 4:17.

4. According to James 4:17 and Proverbs 6:6–8, how should Christians think about doing less than our best?

_____

_____

_____

_____

5. *After reading these two passages, write out three questions you have about these verses.*

1. _____

_____

_____

2. _____

_____

_____

3. _____

_____

_____

6. *What other verses in the Bible help to answer your questions?*

_____

_____

_____

7. *What do you think is the most important idea of these two passages, James 4:17 and Proverbs 6:6–8?*

_____

_____

_____

8. *What do these verses ask you to think, feel, or do?*

_____

_____

_____

DON'T GET TIRED

> *My son, do not despise the LORD's discipline*
> *or be weary of his reproof,*
> *for the LORD reproves him whom he loves,*
> *as a father the son in whom he delights.*
>
> PROVERBS 3:11–12

When I was a kid, I went on a canoe camping trip with a bunch of other boys. My canoe was so hopelessly slow that we fell way, way, way behind the other boats. Eventually, my canoe mate and I had canoed for so long without seeing anyone else that I was sure we must have rowed by the meeting spot on the riverbank. We got tired, and we thought of quitting, but we both knew that would mean being stuck in the middle of nowhere. We persevered and eventually found the rest of our group. (And I only fell out of the canoe once!)

On your journey ahead, there will be many times when you might be tempted to give up or give in. Life can be really hard. All the verses we've studied and the wisdom God offers you may seem hard when you're faced with a world that seems easy. But persevere in the truth. God has offered humanity one of the greatest gifts imaginable—a relationship with Him. This is only possible because, in Christ, all of our sins can be forgiven, and we can be joined to a Holy God.

I pray you know Him, and in knowing Him, you will love Him, and in loving Him, you will follow Him with every ounce of energy you have in your being from now until eternity. God loves you! Don't forget it. Let that strengthen and encourage you!

1. *How do you know that your mom or dad loves you?*

_____

_____

_____

2. *Do you remember a time where you felt like giving up on something important?*

_____

_____

_____

3. *Why do you think that God "reproves" (or corrects) and disciplines those He loves?*

_____

_____

_____

Read 2 Corinthians 12:9–10.

4. *How do both Proverbs 3:11–12 and 2 Corinthians 12:9–10 encourage believers?*

_____

_____

_____

5. *After reading these two passages, write out three questions you have about these texts.*

1. _____

_____

_____

2. _____

_____

_____

3. _____

_____

_____

6. *What other verses in the Bible help to answer your questions?*

_____

_____

_____

_____

7. *What do you think is the most important idea of these two passages,*
2 Corinthians 12:9–10 and Proverbs 3:11–12?

_____

_____

_____

8. *What do these verses ask you to think, feel, or do?*

_____

_____

_____

_____

ONE MORE THING

There is not a day of your life that you will not have to make decisions. While there are not going to be any "do-overs," you are going to have a lot of opportunities to try again. Christian men and women are blessed by the Word of God, the Bible. God doesn't just tell us what to do and what not to do, He tells us how He feels about us. It is His love for us that drives the wisdom He offers us.

God gives us wisdom like a good parent who gives guidance and correction to a child when they need it so that they won't be harmed and so that they know what to do. Let your love for Him drive the choices you make. You can speak to God right now in prayer, and you can hear from God right now in His Word. I pray that you will grow in your love of the God who has loved you enough to guide you and save you from sin!

A Prayer You Can Say . . .

Heavenly Father,

Please guide my life. Help me to pursue the virtues that will make me wise.

Protect me from the struggles that would separate me from You.

Give me courage to do what is right even if no one around me is following You.

Give me confidence in who You declare me to be.

Let my whole life praise You.

Thank You for loving me and leading me.

In the name of Your Son, Jesus Christ!

Amen.

ACKNOWLEDGMENTS

I'd like to thank Trillia Newbell for inviting me to contribute to this Moody Publishers Bible study series and for casting such a compelling vision for kids to be studying the Bible. I'm also grateful for Catherine Parks and Rebecca McLaughlin, whose studies of Colossians and Mark, respectively, kicked off this series magnificently. Their studies are so good that it made me extra proud to join them as a fellow contributor. A special thanks is due to my editor, Amanda Cleary Eastep, who made some fantastic improvements to the resource you're holding.

Lastly, I couldn't do any of this work without my brilliant, hilarious, and supportive wife, Chelsea Lane. We haven't been married nearly long enough. Let's keep going!